CW0066355S

The original appearance of King William's College (Hansom and Welch, 1830) before the fire of 1844. The college was built on the Hangohill estate with money from the Bishop Barrow fund. The college was built from Castletown limestone from the Scarlett quarry.

THE
ISLE OF MAN
A Pictorial History

William Cubbon (1865-1955) holding the Manx Sword of State, traditionally Olaf Godreson's sword of about 1230. Cubbon, son of a Master Mariner of Port St Mary, worked for the *Manx Examiner* and became Librarian at Douglas in 1912. His scholarly *Bibliography of the Isle of Man* is a basic source for Manx history.

THE
ISLE OF MAN
A Pictorial History

D. Robert Elleray, A.L.A.
Fellow of the Royal Society of Arts

Phillimore

1989

Published by
PHILLIMORE & CO. LTD.
Shopwyke Hall, Chichester, Sussex

© D. Robert Elleray, 1989

ISBN 0 85033 677 5

Printed and bound in Great Britain by
BIDDLES LTD.
Guildford, Surrey

For my wife Rosemary (neé Crebbin)
and also Captain Anthony Crebbin and family
of Salamander Bay, New South Wales.

List of Illustrations

Frontispiece: William Cubbon holding the Manx Sword of State

1. The Calf of Man Crucifixion
2. Illustration of Tynwald Hill, 1787
3. Robert Morden's map of the Isle of Man, 1695
4. James Stanley, Lord of Man 1702-36
5. Thomas Wilson
6. Sculpture of the Legs of Man by Bryan Kneale
7. A Manx Cat
8. Cashtal Yn Ard, Maughold
9. Stone crosses at Onchan church
10. Odd's cross, Old Kirk, Braddan
11. Maughold church and cross
12. 'Cross house', Maughold
13. Remains of St Trinian's chapel
14. Early 19th-century view of Castletown
15. Remains of Rushen Abbey
16. The 'Crossag' at Ballasalla
17. Herman Moll's map of the Isle of Man
18. Castle Rushen, Castletown
19. St Mary's chapel and Grammar School, Castletown
20. Old House of Keys, Castletown
21. Satirical illustration of deliberations in the House of Keys
22. Castletown Square
23. Baillie Scott's police station, Castletown
24. Castletown harbour
25. Remains of Castletown windmill
26. King William's College
27. Thomas E. Brown
28. Port St Mary harbour, *c.*1900
29. Cregneish
30. Crebbin's cottage, Cregneish
31. The Chicken Rock lighthouse, *c.*1875
32. View across Port Erin Bay, *c.*1900
33. Victorian view of Port Erin Bay
34. Professor Edward Forbes
35. The *Falcon's Nest Hotel*, Port Erin
36. Port Erin railway station
37. Kirk Rushen (Holy Trinity) and vicarage, near Port Erin
38. Tynwald ceremony at St John's, 5 July 1913
39. Tynwald Fair at St John's, *c.*1905
40. Glen Helen and Rhenass waterfall
41. View of Foxdale mines, *c.*1890

Peel

42. Late 18th-century print of St Patrick's Isle
43. Peel Castle
44. The Round Tower on St Patrick's Isle
45. Ruins of St German's Cathedral

46. Edwardian view of Shore Road
47. Peel fishermen, *c.*1895
48. Peel fishermen and catch, early 20th century
49. The Ward Library, opened 1907
50. Remains of the church of St Peter
51. Former Primitive Methodist chapel, Christian Street
52. Art Nouveau railway station
53. Internees at Peel Camp in 1943
54. The annual Viking race in Peel Bay
55. Kirk Michael
56. Bishop's Court
57. Sulby village
58. New Ballaugh church
59. The Advanced Airship Corporation's hangar near Jurby airfield
60. St Patrick's church, Jurby
61. Kirk Andreas
62. The church at Bride

Ramsey

63. Point of Ayre lighthouse
64. Pierrot show on the beach
65. South Promenade, *c.*1908
66. The old Town Hall, Parliament Street
67. The Market Place and St Paul's church
68. The Plaza cinema
69. The Manx Electric Railway station, Albert Road
70. Roman Catholic church of Our Lady of the Sea
71. Waterloo Road Methodist chapel
72. View of the Mooragh Promenade
73. Boating on the Sulby River, *c.*1905
74. The Laxey Wheel
75. An 1890 advertisement for Laxey Glen
76. Open air dancing at Laxey Glen gardens, *c.*1914

Douglas

77. Royal Mail Packet steamer *Tynwald*, *c.*1840
78. Douglas Harbour and Bay from Douglas Head
79. Douglas Head lighthouse, about 1900
80. Marine Drive Gateway
81. The steamship *Mona*, early 20th century
82. Sail and steam boats in Douglas Harbour, about 1900
83. Douglas Harbour and Pier
84. The *Empress Queen*, *c.*1913
85. Victoria Pier, about 1900
86. Sir William Hillary

87. The Tower of Refuge
88. R.N.L.I. centenary celebrations on
    10 May 1932
89. The ferry *Peveril*
90. St George's church
91. Old St Matthew's church
92. The *Castle Mona Hotel*
93. Oddfellow Hall, Athol Street
94. The Manx Government Office, Prospect Hill
95. Henry Brougham Loch and his family
96. National Westminster Bank building,
    Prospect Hill
97. Town Hall, Ridgeway Street
98. Manx Museum building, Crellin's Hill
99. Extension to the Manx Museum nearing
    completion
100. Loch Promenade, *c*.1910
101. The *Villiers Hotel*, Loch Promenade
102. Late Victorian beach scene, Douglas Bay
103. Gale in Douglas Bay
104. Pre-First World War view from Douglas
     Head
105. Victorian boarding house advertisement for
     Earle House
106. Okell's Falcon Brewery, Falcon Street
107. Roman Catholic church Our Lady of the Isle
108. Villas on the east side of Finch Road
109. Elegant doorway, Mount Pleasant
110. Woodburn Square and Hawarden Avenue
111. Advertisement, by the architect
     W. J. Rennison, *c*.1885
112. Demesne Road, Upper Douglas
113. Trinity Methodist church, Bucks Road, and
     the *Rosemount Hotel*
114. Destruction of a Mount Havelock terrace,
     August 1988
115. The Gaiety Theatre
116. Programme for the opening of the Gaiety
     Theatre
117. Plaster figure inside the Gaiety Theatre
118. The Palace entertainment centre, Queen's
     Promenade
119. Interior of the Palace Ballroom, *c*.1910
120. Advertisement for the 'Palace and New
     Opera House', *c*.1892
121. The Palace Lido
122. Derby Castle
123. The Villa Marina
124. Facade of the Strand Cinema
125. Strand (originally Sand) Street
126. The Royalty Cinema, Walpole Avenue
127. Advertisement for the Royalty Cinema,
     c.1932
128. The Crescent cinema on the seafront
129. Cunningham's Holiday Camp
130. Publicity postcard for Cunningham's Camp,
     c.1900
131. Meeting at Belle Vue racecourse

132. Opening of the Isle of Man Railway, 1873
133. Steam train in Douglas station, *c*.1920
134. Electric tram terminus near Derby Castle,
     c.1910
135. View of the Electric Railway terminus
     in 1988
136. Diesel railcars at Douglas station
137. Horse tram depot at Summerland
138. Horse tram
139. Horse changing ends at Victoria Street
140. Electric Railway car no. 2 at Summerland
     terminus
141. The new Tourist Trophy Grandstand,
     Glencrutchery Road
142. Evening practice prior to the 1988 TT races
143. Motor-cycle race circuit on Douglas Bay
     sands, 1988

Braddan
144. Old Kirk Braddan
145. Open air service at new Braddan church,
     c.1920
146. New church at Kirk Braddan

The Nunnery
147. Romney's portrait of Captain
     John Taubman, 1788
148. The Nunnery and Inkerman Obelisk

Onchan
149. Late 19th-century view of Onchan
150. William Bligh
151. Government House

Baillie Scott
152. Mackay Hugh Baillie Scott
153. Baillie Scott's drawing of the Red House,
     Victoria Road
154. The Red House in 1987
155. Village Hall, Onchan
156. Ivydene, Little Switzerland
157. 'Ashfield', Glencrutchery Road
158. The Gelling family, Ashfield House, *c*.1890
159. The second Ashfield House, East Preston,
     Sussex

Manx Miscellany
160. Cooil Methodist chapel
161. Dalrymple Memorial chapel, Union Mills
162. Crosby Methodist chapel
163. Sir Thomas Hall Caine
164. Greeba Castle, Crosby
165. Mr. Hall Caine
166. The *Summit Hotel*, Snaefell
167. Groudle Glen Railway
168. Ballasalla, *c*.1910
169. Ronaldsway airport, 1988

Preface

This book is the result of an enthusiasm for its subject matter – as any book worthy of attention must be – and the desire to communicate a consuming interest to others. My first visit to the Isle of Man in 1985 was at the instigation of my Manx wife who had after many years decided to visit the Island to do some preliminary research into the history of her family – the Crebbins and Gellings. Whilst this work went forward I soon became aware of the unique quality of the Manx people, their history and the physical beauty of the Island, all of which presented an irresistible invitation to compile a concise visual record of the place to serve as an introduction to a fascinating area. Thus, within a limited space, I have attempted to celebrate the 'Manxness of Man', to indicate briefly some of its varied history, the wide range of its architecture and historical personalities – all important strands in the fabric of Manx individuality. Long may this way of life survive, and resist the ever increasing modern trend towards uniformity.

D. Robert Elleray
January 1989

Acknowledgements

First my sincere thanks to Miss A. M. Harrison, B.A., F.S.A., Librarian Archivist at the Manx Museum and Peter Kelly for their invaluable help in my research. I am also grateful to the staff of the Manx Museum Library for their courteous assistance and to John R. Bowring (Douglas Library).

In addition to my own photographs I am grateful to the Manx Museum, Peter Kelly and Mervin Russell Stokes (Manager of the Gaiety Theatre), for permission to reproduce items from their collections. Photographic work, including the jacket illustration, was carried out by Mike Kelly, of Onchan, and the manuscript was typed by Esme Evans B.A., A.L.A.

The photographs used as the frontispiece and plates 5, 8, 27, 31, 33, 34, 38, 41, 47, 53, 63, 77, 88, 90, 91, 102, 132 and 147 are copyright of the Manx Museum.

... I sailed from Whitehaven in one of his Majesty's Cutters; and, as the day was delightfully serene, in a few hours observed the mountains of Mona breaking from the ambient clouds. On a nearer approach they afforded us a sublime and picturesque view: Mountain piled upon mountain, extending in a lofty range for many miles; in the centre of which, Snaffield, with awful grandeur, lifted his brow to Heaven, and seemed proudly to claim the pre-eminence.

David Robertson, *A Tour through the Isle of Man*, 1794.

A Glance at Manx History

Like many islands, the Isle of Man owes much of its charm and special character to geographical remoteness which during a long history has ensured a degree of protection from the more uniform development of mainland areas and allowed a sturdy individualism to flourish. In fact, it was the position of the Island in the centre of the northern Irish Sea that led to the name Man – probably deriving from Vannin or Mannin, the Manx for middle, that is between England and Ireland.

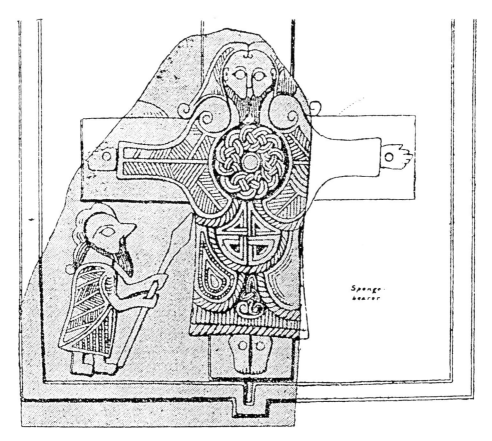

Sponge-bearer

1. The Calf of Man Crucifixion is a unique example of Celtic art of the late eighth century. The style derives from the eastern Mediterranean and was possibly part of an altar. The fragment was discovered in 1773, and purchased in 1956 for display in the Manx Museum.

The earliest people to occupy Man, probably from northern France, arrived in the Middle Stone Age *c*.3500 B.C. During this period and the later Neolithic, Bronze and Iron Ages, cultivation began and burial sites like Meayll Hill Circle, Giant's Grave (St John's) and Cronk ny Irree Laa (Dalby), appeared. Further settlements by peoples from Germany and the Low Countries via England took place, and around 200 B.C., Celtic Iron Age immigrants arrived and built hill forts such as Balladoole, Cronk

Sumark, Arbory and Braddan. Following these troubled times the Roman invasion of Britain brought comparative peace, although the Romans themselves never settled on the Island they named Mona. By the fifth century A.D., when Christianity reached the Isle of Man, the pattern of Celtic culture was established with considerable Irish influence, and a Gaelic language, 'Manx', developed,[1]and was widely spoken until the late 19th century.[2] Recent attempts to revive the language have formed part of a new awareness of Manx identity.

Missionaries from Ireland arrived in the fifth century, possibly St Patrick himself who is said to have founded a church on St Patrick's Isle, Peel, in 477. Later Germanus established a small cruciform church, St German's Cathedral, on the same site. Other missionaries followed whose names have influenced place names on Man – MacCuill (Maughold), St Brigid (Bride), St Andrew (Andreas), and St Ronan (Marown). At this time small rectangular chapels, called *Keeills*,[3] combined with homesteads, formed the basic architecture and land divisions, the *udal* system, where each unit, the *treen*, was administered by a chieftain. Evidence suggests that this early Celtic Christian period was one of stability which continued until the disruptive Norse invasions. The most outstanding survivals of the early Christian period on Man were the carved stone crosses which form a distinctive contribution to Celtic antiquities. Along with the 'ogham' burial inscriptions (fifth to sixth centuries), the crosses provide historical evidence illustrating the evolution of Celtic art. The tradition of the Manx cross was continued by the Norsemen and beyond into medieval times.

The Norse Invasions

In 798 the relative peace of the Island was broken by the arrival of the Vikings who for many years subjected the inhabitants to constant fear of raiding and plunder. After some fifty years the Vikings began to settle in the northern plain where the fertile land around Andreas attracted colonisation leading to exploitation and seizure of the Celtic homesteads. The extension of Norse influence to the Isle of Man was part of an occupation of Orkney and Shetland (the 'Nordreys') and the Hebrides (the 'Sudreys') by the Scandinavians in the ninth century. This culminated in the establishment of Norse rule in the Island by Godred Crovan (son of Harold the Black, called King Orry, from Iceland) following his defeat of the Manx at the battle of Sky Hill (Scacafell near Ramsey) in 1079. Norse rule continued from 1079 to 1265 and was of profound importance to the creation of Manx identity and the long tradition of independent government.

As the Norse settlers integrated with the islanders and were converted to Christianity, they replaced the Celtic tribal government with their own annual assembly of freemen, the *Thing*, where general business was dealt with, laws published and disputes settled. The assembly was held at a designated site, *völlr*, and the gathering was known as *Thingvöllr*. The name was later changed to 'Tynwald', and still meets at Tynwald Hill, St John's, every year on 5 July (old Midsummer's Day), making it the oldest parliament in the world with an unbroken tradition. Tynwald, therefore, is quintessential to the concept of Manx identity and underlines the importance of the Viking element in Manx history. Today the Court of Tynwald consists of a Governor appointed by the crown;[4] a Legislative Council composed of the Bishop of Sodor and Man, Attorney-General and eight members selected by the House of Keys; and the House of Keys which is a representative assembly of 24 members chosen by a system of adult suffrage.

The Kingdom of Man continued after Crovan's death in 1095 until 1265 when the last Norse King, Magnus, died at Castle Rushen. In 1265 when King Haakon of Norway was defeated by Alexander III of Scotland at the battle of Largs, Magnus declared allegiance to Alexander. This ushered in a short and unsettled period of Scottish rule until 1333, when Edward III took the Island and began the line of English Lords of Man.

The Stanleys and After

2. The ancient and historic Tynwald Hill, St John's, from an illustration in Grose's *Antiquities* (1787). The terraced 'hill', possibly a Bronze Age burial mound, became the site of the Viking assembly, the Thingvöllr, *c*.870. It is linked by a processional path to a courthouse site, occupied since 1704 by St John's chapel (rebuilt 1849).

Initially English rule in Man maintained a feudal society with the Manx as tenants. But, despite this, Tynwald continued and once the Stanleys were granted the Lordship of Man by Henry IV in 1405, a more enlightened administration was introduced. Sir John Stanley II (ruled 1414-37) made important reforms at the 1423 Tynwald at Castletown. The 'Manx Magna Carta' instigated written records of laws adopted and established a jury system to settle disputes. James Stanley I, 7th Earl Derby (ruled 1627-51), became the most popular of the line, earning the title 'Y Stanlagh Moar' – the Great Stanley. Later, however, there were revolts against English authority when Illiam Dohne became a popular hero and focus for discontent. He was executed in 1663. The last Stanley was James II, 10th Earl Derby (ruled 1702-36), on whose death the Lordship passed to a distant relative, James Murray, 2nd Duke of Atholl.

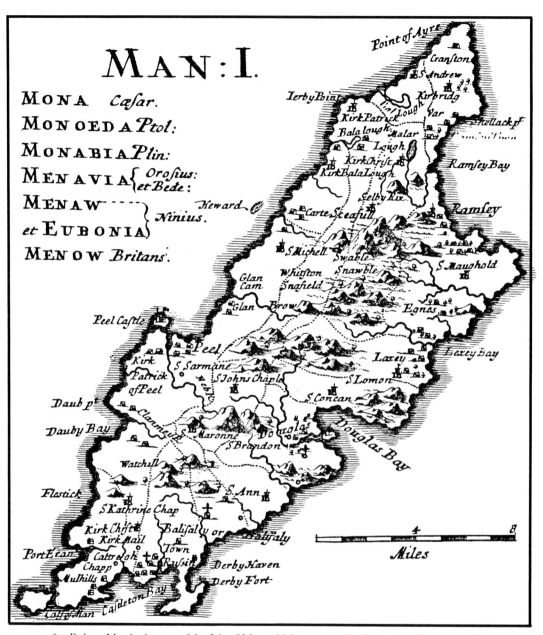

MAN: I.

MONA Cæsar.
MONOEDA Ptol:
MONABIA Plin:
MENAVIA { Orosius: et Bede:
MENAW ----- } Ninius.
et EUBONIA }
Heward ◎
MENOW Britans'.

3. Robert Morden's map of the Isle of Man which appeared in Camden's *Britannia*, 1695.

James Murray took his responsibilities seriously and his appointment was greeted with general acclaim on his arrival at Castle Rushen. The next Tynwald Day the Duke proceeded to St John's where he presided over the assembly with great pageantry, an event not repeated until the visit of George VI in July 1945. Within a year of his becoming Lord of Man, Murray proved his sincerity by granting reforms amounting to a Bill of Rights for the Manx people. A prolonged crisis over widespread smuggling marred these benefits, however, and led Britain to stop the wholesale evasion of customs duties and the use of the Island as an illegal depot for goods. Action was taken on Murray's death in 1764, and negotiations were begun with his joint successors for the purchase of the rights. The Atholls were naturally unwilling to make concessions and the affair was aggravated by Parliament passing the Mischief Act in 1765, which allowed British revenuemen the right of search by land and sea. The Atholls gave way and protests by the Islanders were ignored. C.W. Airne describes the outcome:[5] 'The Duke claimed a large sum for the surrender of all his rights, but Britain, prepared to purchase the regalities only, offered but £70,000, to which a joint annuity of £2,000 was later added. The Atholls demurred, but had to submit. In 1765, the Revestment Act ended the Atholl Lordship. The King's Majesty of England, George III, became the first Regal Lord of Man.'

4. James Stanley, 10th Earl of Derby, Lord of Man 1702-1736, and sometime Mayor of Liverpool. On his death without surviving children the Lordship passed to a distant relation, John Murray's son, James, 2nd Duke of Atholl.

Although the 3rd Duke allowed his claims to full compensation to lapse, his son, John Murray, 4th Duke of Atholl, renewed the grievance and, after repeated efforts, the crown relented and appointed the Duke Governor-General of Man in 1793. Murray's self interest and nepotism soon made him extremely unpopular and led to widespread unrest and rioting which drove him from Man in 1825. Three years later the Crown decided to purchase the Duke's remaining rights. This resulted in a very generous settlement of over £417,000, although this sum was more than recuperated by the Treasury's retention of the Island's surplus revenue until 1866.

In the 1860s the seat of government was transferred from Castletown to Douglas, in acknowledgement of the rapid growth and importance of Douglas both commercially and as a successful resort. In 1863 a period of positive and popular governorship began under Lord Loch, who improved financial arrangements with the Treasury which benefited the Isle of Man. In 1866 the House of Keys Election Act introduced the democratic ideal of election by popular franchise.

The latter part of the 19th century brought prosperity through the 'Visiting Industry' when Ramsey, Port Erin, Port St Mary, and Peel all joined Douglas as tourist resorts. The resulting demand for transport led initially to the formation of the Isle of Man

Steam Packet Company, and later to the introduction of steam and electric railways and horse-drawn trams which happily survive today and continue to provide both interest and pleasure to tourists. In 1828 the Isle of Man Mining Company was formed to exploit the Island's natural resources of metals, and in 1854 the famous Laxey Wheel pumping engine was opened.

Throughout the 19th century the sea continued to play a vital part in Manx life. Shipbuilding was an established activity in many places and the preserved ship *Peggy*, made for George Quayle in 1789, may be seen at the Nautical Museum in Castletown. In 1826 the Bath Yard re-opened in Douglas and soon launched the largest ship so far built on the Island, the *Columbine* (200 tons). This led to renewed shipbuilding activity and other yards set up at Ramsey in 1832 and Peel the following year. The boom was largely due to the low duty on imported timber which continued until 1866. In 1835 the *Orleana* (650 tons) was launched at the Bath Yard, and in 1841 the passenger vessel *King Orry* was built for the Isle of Man Steam Packet Company. During these years boats were built for the Australia run including the *Yarra-yarra* by Qualtrough & Co., and the *Vixen* by Graves of Peel. Boats for the local fishing fleets, the 'nickeys' and 'nobbies',[6] were also produced, although by 1900 both the fishing and coastal trade had declined considerably,[7] and this decline has continued.

Tourism continued to dominate the Island's economy as it moved into the present century. Beginning with modest annual visitations of some 25,000 in the 1830s, the total rose rapidly thereafter to about 60,000 in the 1860s, 90,000 in 1873, 180,000 in 1884, and 348,000 in 1887. In 1913 over 600,000 visitors came to the Island, a total only exceeded during the post World War Two boom year, 1948, when visitors numbered 625,000. Since then there has been a decline, no doubt reflecting the intense competition in the wider tourist industry and the attraction of cheaper continental holidays. The Manx response to the slump was the Report of a Commission set up in 1955 to investigate possible ways of improving and modernising tourist facilities. To some it would seem that the Report's recommendations, outlined in *Visiting Industry*, attempted to reconcile contradictory aims: to modernise, whilst still retaining and enhancing the traditional Manx scene – a dilemma by no means unique to the Isle of Man.

However, there were benefits from the 1955 Report – the opening of the wildlife park at Ballaugh, the new passenger terminal at Douglas and the purchase by the government of the Laxey Wheel and the Gaiety Theatre, thus ensuring their restoration and survival. Other changes included the introduction of car ferries in 1962, a casino, and the Summerland Leisure Centre in 1973. In 1970 a further *Tourist Industry Development Report* was published, concentrating on the need for more holiday accommodation. But the related issue of conserving the 19th- and early 20th-century architectural heritage of Douglas and other towns has yet to be properly addressed and should logically go hand in hand with the admirable policy of preserving the 'Manxness of Man'. In 1986 visitors numbered 340,000, and tourism contributed 11% of the national income compared with about 12% for manufacture. At present, the rapid growth of the financial sector, representing 30% of income, seems more likely to cause radical changes in the Isle of Man than any attempt to stimulate tourism.

The Church in the Isle of Man

The Church has played a leading part in Manx history and, like Tynwald, expresses an important aspect of the innate independence of Manx institutions. The Diocese of Sodor and Man was formed in about 1066 and included the Hebrides, but was for a time suffragan to Trondheim, later joining the Province of York in 1542. The original cathedral of St German's (c.1235) on St Patrick's Isle, Peel, has been ruinous since 1772 and subsequently the chapel[8] at Bishopscourt served as a pro-cathedral until the parish church of St German (1879) became a cathedral church in 1980. The Diocese has its own convocation and the Bishop, who is a member of the Court of Tynwald, can also sit but not vote in the House of Lords. The most distinguished Manx Bishop was Thomas Wilson (1663-1755), who proved a great reformer of Manx spiritual life, and worked closely with James Stanley, 10th Earl of Derby, to improve the welfare, education and industries in the Island.

Both Wilson and his successor Mark Hildesley (1698-1772) were energetic church builders and restorers, providing St Mary's Castletown (1701), followed by Lezayre, St Matthew's Douglas, Kirk Michael and others. John Betjeman asserts that Manx churches are 'many and small – though none of the earlier ones have much architectural distinction, they a have storm-resisting, prayer-soaked holiness

5. Thomas Wilson (1663-1755) from Burton, Cheshire, who attended Trinity College, Dublin, and was ordained priest in 1686. As chaplain to the 9th Earl of Derby he was persuaded to accept the See of Sodor and Man and was consecrated Bishop in 1698 at Peel. Wilson proved an assiduous reformer of spiritual standards in Man and built several churches.

about them', a very appropriate description of churches such as Kirk Malew, Maughold and old Ballaugh. But not all are humble. The Gothic Revival produced some good buildings such as J.L. Pearson's Kirk Braddan and St Matthew's, Doulglas; Henry Clutton's St Mary of the Isle, Douglas (Roman Catholic); the Manx architect Ewan Christian's St Thomas, Douglas, and later St Ninian's, Douglas, by Caroe; and Scott's Our Lady of the Sea (Roman Catholic) at Ramsey. These buildings mark a notable contribution to Manx church building by leading British architects. Nonconformity, especially Methodism, has also provided several fine buildings such as the Waterloo chapel at Ramsey and the Primitive Methodist chapel, Christian Road, Peel. Sadly, the best, the Victoria Street Methodist, Douglas, has been demolished, and the Presbyterian Church, Finch Road, mutilated – the tower and spire surviving as a lift shaft to a modern office block! Anglican losses have been St Peter's, Peel; St Barnabas, Fort Street, Douglas; and the conversion into offices of St Mary's, Castletown, with the loss of monuments and a unique box-pewed interior.

Douglas and its Architecture

The first visitors to the Isle of Man came in search of scenery, a bracing climate and good sea bathing. In the words of Richard Townley[9] in 1789, 'great numbers of strangers are visiting this island, either for pleasure, curiosity, or the hopes of recovering lost health'. But it was David Robertson's *A Tour through the Isle of Man* (1794 and later published in French and German) which played a leading part in attracting tourists to the Island towards the end of the 18th century and indicating the scenic pre-eminence of Douglas Bay. So, popularity increased, but for some time the initial problem of how to reach Man remained: the success of tourism hinged upon efficient sea transport, this being established from about 1820. As steamships and mainland railways improved, the Isle of Man was in an ideal position to benefit from the multitudes of holiday makers at last able to escape from the grim northern industrial towns. The resulting boom was remarkable and sustained. It created Douglas as we now know it.

The chief asset Douglas has as a resort is its fine setting ranking among the best in Britain and comparing favourably with Scarborough, Hastings, Llandudno or Eastbourne. H.A. Bullock,[10] writing in 1816, remarked 'The approach ... by sea presents a most inspiring aspect ... the semi-circle of the bay ... takes in at once a variety of objects calculated to arise fairy hopes of the interior'. John Warwick Smith's series of watercolours[11] of the Island, painted for the Duke of Atholl, fully confirm Bullock's 'fairy hopes'.

By 1800 a small cramped town had developed to the north of Douglas harbour and was providing, according to Richard Townley, reasonable accommodation with some theatrical diversions and simple entertainment. Two assembly rooms were functioning by about 1780, in Fort Street and near the Parade on North Quay, and by 1810 Banks Dancing Room and Playhouse existed near the Lake Brewery. By the time Robert Haining published his guide book to the Island in 1822, fairly regular steamboat services were operating and 'considerable preparation [was being] made for ... visitors by enlarging the inns and increasing the number of lodging houses'. Haining estimated the annual number of visitors at about 3,000 and, in 1832, nine hotels and 32 lodging houses were listed. By 1843 another guide[12] described Douglas: 'There is no watering place in the United Kingdom where there is better accommodation ... or where more respect is paid, or greater civility, liberality and attention shown ...' The traditional warmth and courtesy of the Manx people was certainly beginning to be appreciated by visitors. After 1850 the influx of visitors became a flood, reflecting the increasing affluence and mobility of working people of the industrial north. The introduction of the August 'Bank Holiday' in 1871 led to the growth of all seaside resorts. During this boom Douglas remained pre-eminent although by the 1890s other resorts had developed. A Victorian seafront appeared at Port Erin, with little or nothing behind it, until the dreary housing estates arose this century. At Ramsey a grand holiday scheme, the Mooragh Promenade backed by a large pleasure park with boating lake, was opened in 1887 but the seafront was never finished and, despite plans for infill completion, still retains an awkward gap-toothed appearance.

With the possible exception of Port Erin, it was only in Douglas that the requirements of visitors really influenced the town's architectural and social identity. During the first half of the 19th century the Isle of Man benefited from the work of two architects, John Welch and John Robinson (1798-1880) who, together with John Taggart, a prolific builder architect, furnished the Island with many of its most characteristic buildings. Welch arrived in 1810 and was associated with the Hansom family of architects, and also wrote a guide to the Island.[13] He soon became an important designer of Manx churches in a local gothic style, including Kirk Onchan and St Barnabas (demolished in 1969) in Douglas. He also joined in the castellated vogue seen in his best-known work, the Tower of Refuge erected in 1832, whose detail is echoed in stone and stucco in many Manx buildings. The influence of Robinson, who had arrived in 1789 to carry out work at the Nunnery, is seen in Welch's later designs and develops into a general style of building adopted by James Cowle, George Kay, and the prolific Rennisons, whose hotels and houses such as Falcon Cliff and Derby Castle (demolished) became part of the Manx 19th-century scene.

John Robinson,[14] although self-taught, brought a more sophisticated style, Nash-inspired, and an awareness of Regency town planning. It is to his work and influence during the early to mid-19th century that Douglas owes much of its finest buildings and estates. Of these the Oddfellows Hall (now Law Courts) in Athol Street is outstanding and the Bank of Mona, now the House of Keys, remains a delightful essay in stucco Italianate. The gothic element remained, however, and Robinson was at ease in styles both Romantic and Classical.

The increasing pressure for accommodation in Douglas during the mid-19th century led to large-scale housing developments centred on the Christian Buck Estate, comprising Finch Road to Christian Road down to Mount Havelock, and including Mona Terrace and Albert and Mona Streets. An official stone-laying by William Finch Christian took place in 1854 for the Finch Hill Estate, and it is the line of large gabled villas in Finch Road which form the climax of the Regency phase of the town's growth: these are in no way derivative but form a highly original contribution to Regency architecture. It is incredible that this area of special architectural character has just been dealt a grievous blow by the demolition (1988) of the central range of Robinson's Regency terrace on Mount Havelock, together with the old St Barnabas Vicarage at the bottom of Christian Road. This outstanding Regency area continues with several fine terraces – Mona, Windsor, Albert, Osborne and Cambridge, together with Derby and Woodbourne Squares. Continuing along Woodbourne Road there is an extraordinary variety of later 19th-century buildings, including several fine villas and groups of houses.

As the tourist industry reached its climax toward the close of the Victorian period, the ever increasing demand for boarding house accommodation led to mass production of buildings following standard patterns each with neat stucco facade combining drip mouldings, standard doorways and surmounted by faced dormers, all deriving from the estate styles and forming some handsome streets such as Demesne and Selborne Roads, Hawarden Avenue and several more. These styles were repeated in other parts of the Island, particularly in Port Erin, and often in rural villas and public houses. Under the benign administration of Governor Loch it was decided to create a formal seafront for Douglas, a move which led to the erection of the Loch and Harris Promenades and Victoria Street. The construction began in 1875 and gave the town one of the finest promenades in Europe, and one meriting careful protection. Sadly, however, the southern range of the Loch section, although in good condition and including the once prestigious *Villiers Hotel*, is now threatened with demolition to make way for a leisure complex.

An important episode in Manx architectural history began in 1889 when the English architect Baillie Scott arrived in Douglas from Bath and started work with a local Surveyor, Fred Saunderson, in Athol Street, before setting up himself in 1893. Scott was influenced by Voysey, the Arts and Craft Movement and Chester Tudor Revival. His attendance at the Douglas School of Art and his contact there with Archibald Knox led to joint Art Nouveau decoration schemes in several local houses. The result was a notable flowering of Art Nouveau housing in the Onchan area which also included work by Armitage Rigby and R.F. Douglas, and had considerable influence on Douglas house design beyond 1900. Chief among Scott's designs exemplifying the 'English Domestic Revival' are *Oakleigh* in Glencrutchery Road, *Ivydene* in Little Switzerland, and his own residence, *The Red House*,[15] in Victoria Road (1892-93). Later he worked with Saunderson on the Onchan Bay Estate, and in 1887-98 designed the stylish and influential Onchan Village Hall. In 1900 Scott designed Castletown Police Station in a medieval style that would have gained the approval of both Welch and Robinson. Competing with Scott was Armitage Rigby, whose commissions included the *British Hotel*, North Quay, Douglas, the elaborate lych gate at Kirk Michael and extensive restoration work at Castle Rushen.

Baillie Scott left Douglas to practise in Bedford in 1901, and the town continued to expand its entertainment facilities for visitors, but it had been the skill and enterprise of architects like Robinson, Rennison, Cowle, Baillie Scott and others that had transformed Douglas from the small, cramped port of the early 19th century into a town of great architectural variety and character, an important part of the Manx heritage.

The first decade of the present century saw no slackening in the tourist trade and Douglas harbour, 'the gateway to the Island', underwent considerable change. The Victorian pier had been enlarged by 1890, and the old Red Pier (1832) was extended to form a new structure, the King Edward VIII Pier, during the 1930s. In 1913 'a magnificent Kursaal', the Villa Marina, providing a large concert hall, gardens and other facilities, was opened by Lord and Lady Raglan on a site formerly occupied by Marina Lodge. This new development and the widening of the Loch Promenade, together with several cinemas, made up the bulk of public building until 1939. The architect Harry Lomas, employing the white tile Art Deco style, designed the Royalty, Walpole Avenue, the Crescent on the sea front and probably the delightful new facade of the Strand Cinema. Today no cinemas remain open on the Island although there are plans to open one in the Summerland complex. Despite the seasonal fluctuation of population experienced in the resorts, the figure for Douglas has remained fairly steady for several years at about 20,000. However, some urban growth has taken place beginning with Pulrose, Onchan, Bray Hill (garden city style), and more recently Birch Hill and Willaston, where a College of Further Education has been established. Housing on the Castletown road, together with an industrial estate at Spring Valley, now begins to menace the hamlet of Cooil and also the Dhoo valley at Braddan between the Peel and Strang roads.

Resulting from the *Visiting Industry Reports*, a large Sea Terminal opened in 1965 and a number of other projects were begun. Of these, the Summerland Leisure Complex opened in 1971 and replaced the group of traditional seaside buildings at Derby Castle with a triumphant display of concrete brutalism – an environmental shock from which the northern end of Douglas Bay may well never recover. In the immediate vicinity of the Palace Lido, the new Casino buildings, again in heartless concrete, have a similar jarring effect emphasising how damaging unsympathetic infilling of sites can be within a context of established traditional architecture, especially in Douglas.

6. The striking metal sculpture of the Legs of Man by Bryan Kneale, stands just outside the airport terminal at Ronaldsway. It was unveiled by Princess Michael of Kent in September 1979.

7. The two characteristic Manx images are the Three Legs and the Manx Cat. The tail-less cat is a mutation preserved by human selection, and in 1964 an official Cattery was established in Nobles Park, Douglas, to ensure protection. Mixed litters occur with normal tails, short tails –' stumpies', and no tails – 'rumpies'.

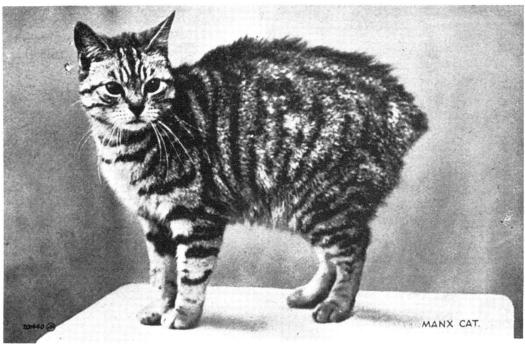

MANX CAT.

The most striking phenomenon in recent Manx history is the rise of banking and finance which seem about to rival the traditional staple industry of tourism. That such an opportunity has presented itself to the Manx people is reason for satisfaction both in the Island and for all sympathetic to the individuality and independence of the Manx nation. Predictably, the pressures on the Manx environment caused by this upsurge are already apparent, especially in Douglas.

Looking to the future, there is every reason to suppose that the Isle of Man will stay true to its centuries-old traditions and remain Manx. Though many northern and midland English have bought retirement homes, this transient population has little or no long-term demographic effect and the island has not attracted the multi-cultural emigration that has affected so much of the mainland. Celt, Norse and Saxon genes still mix in an insular culture that seems set to survive into the future, increasingly aware of the richness and importance of its island heritage.

References

1. No literature resulted but *The Book of Common Prayer* was translated into Manx by Bishop Phillips in 1610. Bishop Wilson published his *Principles and Duties* in Manx (1707) and translated the Bible in 1772-73.
2. Manx was spoken by nearly the whole Island in 1764 (S.P.C.K. Pamphlet), and in 1875 12,350 out of 41,000 spoke Manx. This had fallen to 165 in 1961 (*see* H.S. Corran, *Isle of Man*, p.83).
3. Nearly 200 keeills are known to have existed. Originally constructed of sods and later of stone with thatched roofs. Remains of keeills survive at Marown, Arbory and Maughold etc.
4. The Lieutenant-Governor represents the Lord of Man, the British Sovereign, and is initially sworn in at Castle Rushen.
5. *The Story of the Isle of Man*, vol. 2, 1964, p.114.
6. Local names for fishing boats. The Nickeys were Cornish-style craft.
7. In 1864 the fleet comprised 290 Manx, 300 Cornish and Scots, and 100 Irish. By 1914 there were only 57 Manx boats, and in 1973 five. Since the war, escallop fishing has become important.
8. By Ewan Christian.
9. Diary kept during a year's stay.
10. *History of the Isle of Man*, p.203-4.
11. The 26 paintings can be seen in the Manx Museum.
12. *A New Guide and Visitors Companion Through the Isle of Man*, p.76.
13. *A Six Day Tour of the Isle of Man by a Stranger*, 1836.
14. *See* Peter Kelly's article in *Manx Life*, Sept.-Oct. 1983, pp.41-44.
15. The best preserved of Scott's houses, and lovingly cared for by its present owners, Mr. and Mrs. J.A. Ranscombe.

Glossary of Manx Words

Balla: Farm or homestead.
Chiollagh: Open hearth.
Cronk: Hill.
Cushag: Ragwort, the Manx national flower.
Deemster: One of the two justices of the Tynwald.
Dhoon: Fort.
Intack: Rough grazing land outside the 'treen'.
Keeill: Small early Christian chapel.
Kerroo: Farmstead.
Keys: *Claves Manniae et Claves Legis* (1417), the Keys of Man and Keys of the Law. The 24 members making up House of Keys, elective branch of the Manx legislature.
Legs of Man: The national badge of Man, of either Sicilian or Scandinavian origin, deriving from the 'Greek cross'. The oldest examples are (1) on the Manx Sword of State (*c*.1250); (2) Maughold Village Cross.
Man: From the Manx *Vannin* or *Mannin*, meaning middle i.e. between England and Ireland. Caesar called Man *Mona*, and Pliny the elder, *Monapia*.
Ogham Script: The alphabet (of 20 characters) used by the ancient Irish and British nations – hence 'ogham stone' thus inscribed.
Quocunque jeceris stabit: 'It will stand wheresoever you throw it'. The motto attached to the Legs of Man, and first used on Manx coins dated 1668.
Sheadings: The Manx electoral divisions. These number six, Ayre, Michael, Garf, Glenfaba, Middle and Rushen, which are subdivided into 17 parishes.
Treen: Land unit of 200-400 acres, subdivided into quarterlands, these usually prefixed with 'Balla'.
Tynwald: Old Norse *Thing-völlr*, field of assembly, the Tynwald Hill at St John's.

Some Dates in Manx History

*c.*200 B.C.	Celtic Iron Age people arrived.
A.D. *c.*430-445	Traditional period for the introduction of Christianity in Man – either by St Ninian (or Trinian), or St Patrick.
798	First Viking raiders arrive.
1066	Refugees from the Norse army defeated at Stamford Bridge arrive in the Isle of Man under Godred Crovan.
1079	Battle of Skyhill. The victor, Godred Crovan, established Norse rule in Man until 1265.
1134	Olaf I founded Cistercian Abbey, Rushen Abbey, near Ballasalla.
1265	King Magnus died at Castle Rushen.
1266	Alexander of Scotland assumes control of Man.
1291	Man comes under English suzerainty.
1310	First use of the three legs symbol by Henry de Bello Morte, Lord of Man.
1333	Man taken by Edward III.
1405	Stanley family rule as Lords of Man commenced, continuing until 1736.
1645	7th Earl of Derby builds Ballachurry Fort (earthwork) for Civil War emergency.
1668	First Manx coinage minted by John Murrey.
1669	Castletown Grammar School founded.
1698	Thomas Wilson consecrated Bishop of Sodor and Man at St German's Cathedral, Peel.
1701	St Mary's, Castletown, consecrated by Bishop Wilson.
1704	Act of Settlement established security of tenure etc.
1707	Bishop Wilson's *Principles and Duties of Christianity*, the 'Manx Catechism', published.
1765	Isle of Man Purchase (Revestment) Act passed.
1771	Isle of Man Harbour and Seaport Act passed.
1773	Calf of Man Crucifixion (eighth-century Manx cross) discovered.
1775	Translation of the Manx Bible completed.
1776	Population of the Island reached 14,027.
1777	John Wesley visited the Isle of Man.
1779	Royal Manx Fencibles raised as an island defence corps.
1781	Captain William Bligh and Miss Elizabeth Betham (of Douglas) married at Kirk Onchan.
1792	The *Manx Mercury*, the first Manx newspaper, printed by Christopher Briscoe.
1808	Lt.-Col. Sir William Hillary (1771-1847), founder of the R.N.L.I., settled at Fort Anne, Douglas.
1822	First guide to the Isle of Man published by Robert Haining.
1825	'Potato riots' erupt against Bishop George Murray, nephew of John Murray, 4th Duke of Atholl.
1828	Formation of the Isle of Man Mining Company.

1829	Isle of Man Steam Packet Company founded.
1830	King William's College established near Castletown.
1841	Launching of the *King Orry* for the Isle of Man Steam Packet Co. at the Bath Yard.
1844	King William's College destroyed by fire.
1847	Queen Victoria and Prince Consort visit the Isle of Man and forced by weather to land at Ramsey instead of Douglas. Albert Tower commemorates this.
1851	Population reached 52,000.
1853	The painter John Martin in the Isle of Man. He died the following year and is buried at Kirk Braddan.
1854	Laxey Wheel, the Lady Isabella, commissioned.
1854	Foundation stone of the Finch Hill Estate laid by William Finch Christian.
1858	Bishop's Court Chapel, designed by Ewan Christian, opened.
1862	Seat of government moved from Castletown to Douglas.
1864	Archibald Knox (d.1933), designer, born at Cronkborne. Taught at Douglas School of Art and knew Baillie Scott.
1865	Governor Loch leased Bemahague for use as Government House.
1866	House of Keys Election Act – the House to be elected by popular franchise.
1869	Iron Pier, designed by J. Dixon, opened opposite the Villa Marina, costing £6,500 (1,000 feet long).
1871	Milner Tower, Bradda Head, erected by public subscription.
1872	Manx Education Act passed.
1873	Isle of Man Railway opened between Douglas and Peel.
1875	Loch Promenade begun, completed in 1878.
1876	Horse tramway introduced on Douglas promenade.
1878	Manx Northern Railway Co. formed opening line from St John's (Peel) to Ramsey.
1879	Isle of Man Natural History and Antiquarian Society formed.
1881	Manx women receive the vote.
1882	Pier, 2,150 feet long, built at Ramsey by Head Wrightson.
1886	Manx Museum and Ancient Monuments Trustees (now Manx Museum and National Trust) established.
1887	Cunningham's Young Men's Holiday Camp founded, the first of its kind.
1889	Architect M.H. Baillie Scott arrived to practise in Douglas.
1892	Manx International Exhibition held at Belle Vue pleasure grounds.
1892	Marine Biological Station established at Port Erin.
1893	First tramway opened in Douglas.
1895	Snaefell Mountain Railway opened.
1896	Douglas Pier dismantled and re-erected at Rhos-on-Sea (demolished 1954).
1900	3 February, Black Saturday, failure of Dumbell's Bank.
1901	Gaiety Theatre opened on July 16.
1902	Edward VII and Queen Alexandra visited the Isle of Man.
1904	First Gordon Bennet Motor Trials held.
1907	28 May, first TT Motor Trials held.
1911	Closure of the Foxdale leadmines.

1914	Motor bus services began in Douglas.
1924	Journal of the Manx Museum began publication.
1927	Island-wide bus services introduced.
1927	Excavation of Viking ship burial at Knock Y Dooney.
1929	George V presented Castle Rushen, Peel Castle and the Tynwald Hill to the Manx people.
1933	Mrs. Christopher Shimmin became first woman member of the Keys.
1937	Calf of Man presented to the Manx National Trust.
1940	Kurt Schwitters (1887-1948), notable German Dadaist painter, interned at the Hutchinson Camp.
1945	George VI and Queen Elizabeth presided at Tynwald.
1948	Largest number of visitors ever to visit the Isle of Man – 625,000.
1955	Visiting Industry Commission Report.
1955	The Queen and Prince Philip visited the Isle of Man.
1957	Snaefell Mountain Railway taken over by Manx Government.
1958	Isle of Man Act passed and MacDermott Commission set up.
1958	Snaefell Mountain Railway *Bungalow Hotel* demolished.
1961	Isle of Man Constitution Act set up Executive Council to advise Governor.
1961	Population 48,113.
1964	Manx Radio began broadcasting.
1965	Douglas sea passenger terminal opened.
1970	Tourist Industry Development Report.
1970	Royal Commission under Lord Kilbrandon on Manx Constitutional position set up.
1971	Summerland holiday centre opened on the site of former Derby Castle.
1973	Summerland Leisure Centre fire disaster.
1976	Population tops 60,000.
1979	Millennium of the Tynwald celebrated.
1979	*Fort Anne Hotel*, landmark and former residence of Sir William Hillary, demolished.
1979	New police headquarters opened in Glencrutchery Road, designed by J.M. Watson.
1982	Excavations at Peel Castle reveal coin hoards and ornaments.
1982	Snaefell Mountain Railway *Summit Hotel* (designed by George Kay) destroyed by fire.
1986	New TT Grandstand opened in Glencrutchery Road, Douglas.
1986	Population 64,282.
1988	Castellated section of Castletown Brewery demolished.
1989	Her Majesty the Queen opens the new extension to the Manx Museum.

8. Cashtal Yn Ard near Maughold, an impressive example of a megalithic chambered cairn, *c*.2000 B.C. The cairn, excavated in 1932-35, has a western forecourt and five compartments where some missing stones have been replaced.

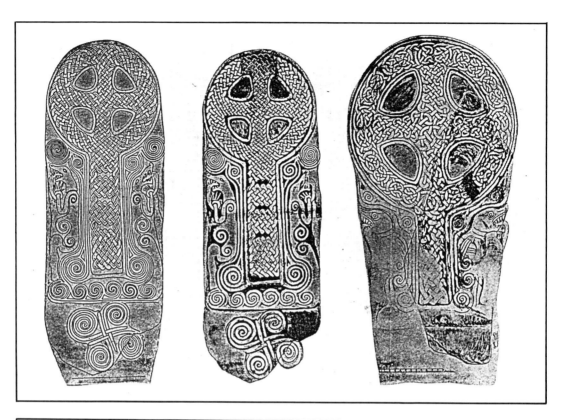

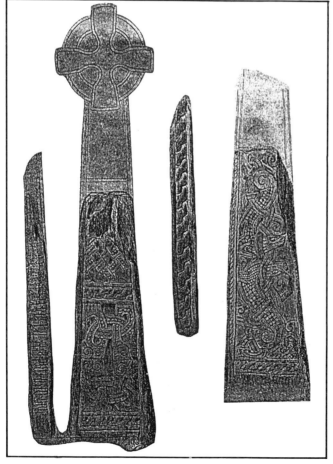

9. Outstanding among the antiquities extant in the Isle of Man are the carved stone crosses, covering a period from *c*.700 to *c*.1300 A.D., and representing both Celtic and Norse craftsmanship. Illustrated here are three zoomorphic crosses preserved at Onchan church.

10. Odd's Cross and fragments at Old Kirk, Braddan. Some 180 carved crosses have been recovered in the Isle of Man and nearly all are now kept in their respective churches – Braddan, Lonan, Maughold, Onchan, Andreas, Jurby and Michael.

11. The remote and ancient Maughold church with the famous cross, one of the two sources for the Three Legs symbol of Man. In the graveyard lies the Manx writer Sir Henry Hall Caine. The view westward from the church towards North Barrule is one of the best in the Island.

12. In 1906 a 'cross house' was opened at Maughold by the Governor, Lord Raglan, to display the collection of Celtic crosses stored at the church.

13. The remains of St Trinian's chapel near Crosby, which once belonged to the Priory of St Ninian, Whithorn, Galloway. The ruin is an enlargement, *c*.1350, of the original structure, *c*.1200, presumably on an ancient Keeil site.

14. Early 19th-century view of Castletown by W. Kinnebrook. To the right of Castle Rushen can be seen the tower of the 'garrison' church of St Mary, with an octagon as the final stage, later removed. In the distance are Cronk ny Arrey Lhaa and South Barrule.

15. A recent view of the remains of Rushen Abbey. Little survives of the cruciform building although the setting near the Silverburn is still an idyllic spot for visitors.

16. The 'Crossag' or Monks' Bridge at Ballasalla, a fine medieval pack-horse bridge spanning the Silverburn near the Cistercian Rushen Abbey.

17. Herman Moll's map of the Isle of Man, dedicated to William Stanley, 9th Earl of Derby, Lord of Man 1672-1701.

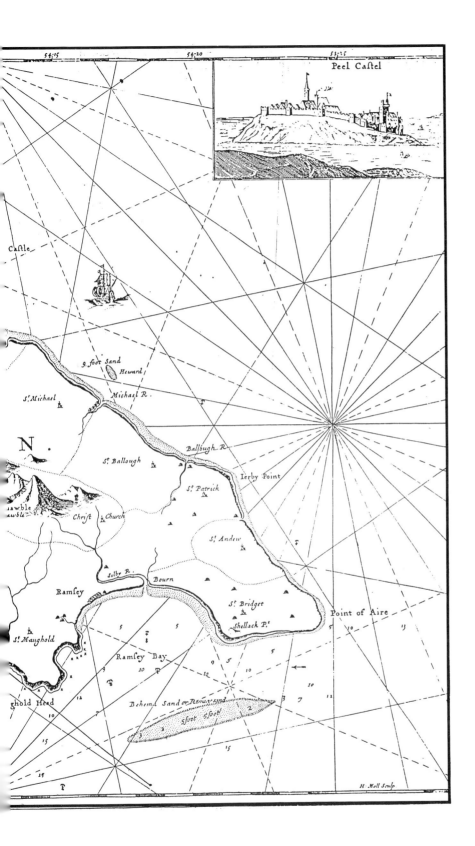

18. Castle Rushen, Castletown, may be considered one of the first and most complete castles in the British Isles. The present building consists largely of 12th- to 14th-century work. The Castle was the seat of Manx government from the Norse period to the 1860s and was carefully restored by Armitage Rigby and others in the late 19th century.

19. St Mary's chapel (arches, left) and Grammar School, Castletown. Built *c*.1220, the chapel was linked to Rushen Abbey until 1540 and continued as the parish church until 1698. School use began in about 1550 and continued until 1930.

20. The old House of Keys, Castletown, now used as a bank. Originally built as a library in 1710 by Bishop Wilson, it was used by the Tynwald Court from 1820 until the main government offices were established on Prospect Hill, Douglas.

21. Satirical illustration by John Stowell depicting deliberations in the House of Keys when it was located in Castletown in the late 18th century.

The Market Place, Castletown, I.O.M.

22. Castletown Square showing the Doric column memorial to Col. Cornelius Smelt, Lieutenant-Governor 1805-32. Beyond is the former St Mary's church designed by Thomas Brine (1826), now refurbished and in commercial use after clearance of its box pews, three-decker pulpit and numerous tablets in 1986.

23. Baillie Scott's baronial-style police station at Castletown, designed in 1901.

24. An attractive group of quayside buildings in Castletown harbour. On the right is the old Isle of Man Steam Packet office.

25. The surviving tower of Castletown windmill (often called the Witches Mill), erected in 1828. The mill, often out of service owing to storm damage, was never a great success and ceased working towards the end of the 19th century.

26. King William's College was founded from a fund established by Bishop Barrow in the late 17th century, the school being opened in 1830. In 1844 a fire necessitated rebuilding in Castletown granite by Hansom and Welch, John Welch being responsible for the central tower, the most distinctive landmark on the Island.

27. The poet and scholar Thomas E. Brown (1830-97), 'the Island's most famous son'. He attended King William's College and was later elected Fellow of Oriel. A Memorial Room in the Manx Museum displays a selection of his memorabilia. Brown is seen here at his old school, c.1892.

28. A variety of craft in Port St Mary harbour in about 1900. The harbour, furnished with two piers, breakwater and lifeboat station, has become a popular centre for sailing holidays.

29. Cregneish, styled 'the most Manx of villages', occupies an idyllic position between Port Erin and the Calf of Man. It includes the National Folk Museum formed in 1938 comprising Harry Kelly's Cottage, the Karran Farmstead and a weaver's cottage, admirably preserving the atmosphere of an upland farming-fishing community *c*.1900.

30. Crebbin's Cottage, one of several thatched buildings in the beautiful village of Cregneish.

31. The Chicken Rock lighthouse is situated two miles south of the Calf of Man and built of Scottish granite which was prepared at Port St Mary and then shipped to the Rock. The photograph shows the tower nearing completion in 1875.

32. View across Port Erin Bay c.1900, showing Bradda Head surmounted by Milner's Tower (1871), erected to the memory of a local benefactor William Milner, a Liverpool safe manufacturer.

OM. PORT ERIN. BRADDA HEAD.

33.   Distant view of Port Erin showing bathing machines and the late Victorian seafront development above the old fishing town.

34. Professor Edward Forbes (1815-54), pioneer marine biologist, was born in Douglas, studied at Edinburgh, and became President of the Geological Society. The rich variety of the Island's marine life led to the founding of the Marine Biological Station at Port Erin in 1842.

35. An old photograph of the *Falcon's Nest Hotel*, Port Erin, showing characteristic stucco crenellation work of the mid-19th century. In 1816 H. A. Bullock described Port Erin as 'a romantic secluded bay, offering an excellent harbour...', qualities leading to limited resort development later in the 19th century.

36.   The Ruabon brick Port Erin railway station, attractively designed to fit a wedge-shaped site. The station has a well preserved booking hall and engine shed, and the nearby Railway Museum exhibits the 0-6-0 *Caledonia*, built for the Foxdale line in 1885, and other interesting items.

37.   Kirk Rushen (Holy Trinity) and vicarage, near Port Erin. The bell turret is a good example of the local style in church building.

38.   Above all, Tynwald is the symbol of Manx independence and is the oldest continuous assembly in the world, dating from Godred Croven in the 11th century. It comprises the Assembly of 24 'Keys' (elected representatives) and the Legislative Council. This picture shows the ceremony at St John's on 5 July 1913, when Lord Raglan was Lieut.-Governor.

Tynwald Fair Day at St. Johns. I. o. M.

39. A crowded scene at the Tynwald Fair at St John's in about 1905.

40. Glen Helen (north of
St John's), with the Rhenass
waterfall, early became a much
frequented beauty spot. The
bridge is now considerably
modified.

41. View of the Foxdale mines,
c.1890. A company was formed
in 1828 and significant
quantities of lead and zinc were
produced until closure in 1911.
A rail link to Peel harbour
opened for mineral traffic in
1886.

Peel

42. Late 18th-century print of St Patrick's Isle, Peel, showing the Round Tower, Castle and St German's Cathedral before its collapse in the 1770s.

43. December calm at Peel Castle. Robertson described it as 'venerable and majestic', but the castle also has a wonderfully romantic presence. The castle was built by William le Scrope, King of Man 1392-99, as a defence for St German's Cathedral.

44. The historic Round Tower dating from the 10th century on St Patrick's Isle, Peel. The tower is of the Irish type, originally with a conical roof, and later modified to a crenellated top.

45. The ruins of St German's Cathedral, Peel. Most of the building dates from the time of Bishop Simon of Argyll who erected the chancel in about 1230. Later repair and extension was carried out in the local red sandstone. The cathedral fell into decay during the 18th century.

46. Edwardian view of Shore Road, Peel, in about 1905. The promenade has superb views of St Patrick's Isle.

47. Fishermen at Peel in about 1895, with St Patrick's Isle as an historic backdrop.

48. Peel fishermen with their catch early this century. Peel, the 'Sunset City', still retains its winding streets and the atmosphere of a fishing port where a kippering industry continues.

49. The Ward Library, Peel, opened in 1907 as a result of the generosity of a rich timber merchant, James Kewley Ward (1819-1910), who emigrated to Canada in 1842 and later became a member of Quebec City Council. Ward was born in Castle Street, Peel, and educated in Douglas.

50. The helm-roof tower and west window surviving from the former church of St Peter, Peel. The church, constructed of the local red Triassic sandstone, was burnt down in 1950.

51. The fine stucco facade of the former Primitive Methodist chapel, Christian Street, Peel. The chapel closed in the 1950s and is now a furniture store.

52. The striking Art Nouveau style railway station at Peel, designed by Armitage Rigby, c.1905. Following closure of the line, the station was re-opened as the Isle of Man Fishermen's Association headquarters in July 1977.

53. Internees at the Peel Camp in 1943. The first camp was established at Ramsey (Mooragh) in May 1940, and others at Douglas and Onchan, with some 14,000 prisoners during the peak period. Among several famous internees were Gerhard Bersu, the archaeologist, and the painter Kurt Schwitters.

54. Holidaymakers watching the annual Viking race held between local crews in Peel Bay in late August.

55. Kirk Michael, rebuilt in 1835 with a large cruciform 'pre-Tractarian' interior. The spacious lych-gate (left) was designed by Armitage Rigby to house the extensive collection of Celtic and Norse crosses, now located inside the church.

PS COURT. SOUTH FRONT, KIRKMICHAEL. ISLE OFMAN. 20037 JV.

56. Bishop's Court, perhaps established by Bishop Symon around 1250, was the customary meeting place for the Manx Convocation. Extensive restorations and additions were carried out by Bishop Wilson and his successors, and a new chapel (right) was added in 1858. In 1979 the building passed into private ownership, breaking an historic Manx tradition.

STATION ROAD, SULBY, ISLE-OF-MAN.

57. Sulby village remains important as the starting point for exploring Sulby Glen, the most spectacular of the glens, referred to by the Victorians as 'the Manx Switzerland'. The Methodist church dates from around 1900.

58. New Ballaugh church (John Welch, 1832) is, according to Betjeman, 'an impressive attempt in local stone to produce Boston Stump reduced in scale'. Unfortunately, the church is now being engulfed by 'superior housing'.

59. The Advanced Airship Corporation's hangar near Jurby airfield, a not altogether welcome intrusion into the impressive landscape of the northern plain.

60. St Patrick's, Jurby, a striking landmark, was rebuilt in 1813 replacing a 13th-century building but using some of its fabric. There is a Norse burial mound in the graveyard and the 'Jurby chalice', a rare pre-Reformation type (1521), is now in the Manx Museum.

61. Kirk Andreas enjoys a wonderfully remote site on the northern plain and contains some fine stone crosses including the Sigurd, Odin and Thorwald crosses. The detached tower was reduced in height around 1900.

62. The church at Bride, rebuilt in 1870, is dedicated to St Brigid, Abbess of Kildare, and stands in the Bride Hills formed from glacial deposits.

63. The remote Point of Ayre lighthouse at the northern tip of the Island was constructed in 1862 by Robert Stevenson. The 103-foot tower, together with the keeper's house, forms a picturesque group.

Ramsey

64. Summer crowds on the beach at Ramsey with a pierrot show in progress (right).

65. South Promenade, Ramsey, crowded with holidaymakers in about 1908. In the mid-1970s this picturesque area was replaced by the Queen's and King's Courts, blocks quite out of character with the historic town.

66. The old Town Hall, Parliament Street, Ramsey, a handsome Victorian building of 1888, was demolished in 1971.

67. Ramsey Market Place with St Paul's church, now overshadowed by the large concrete development (King's Court) and St Paul's Square (right). The church, liberally furnished with galleries, was erected in 1822 and later enlarged.

68. The now disused Plaza cinema, Ramsey. The building is a curious hybrid, an Art Deco foyer having been added to the much older facade of the former Ramsey Palace Ballroom.

69. The remarkably scenic extension of the Manx Electric Railway opened in 1899 and the station, seen here, established in Albert Road. Behind is Quayle's Hall, erected as a Presbyterian church around 1835, and re-opened as a Temperance Hall in 1886.

70. Giles Gilbert Scott's Roman
Catholic church of Our Lady of the Sea at
Ramsey forms, with the adjoining
presbytery, a bold example of Arts and
Crafts Gothic design, utilising stone from
old buildings formerly on the site. The
foundation stone was laid by Bishop
Whiteside of Liverpool in August 1909.

71. The striking classical facade of the
Waterloo Road Methodist chapel,
Ramsey (1845). With seating capacity for
1,000, the chapel claimed to be the largest
on the Island, but the once spacious
interior has now been subdivided.

72. Late Victorian seafront at Ramsey – the Mooragh Promenade, built as part of a new development begun in 1887 and including a pleasure park with boating lake. The terraces were never completed but recently there have been plans to fill the gaps.

73. Boating on the Sulby River near Ramsey in about 1905. The Sulby is the Island's largest river, ten miles in length.

Boating on Sulby River, Ramsey, I.O.M.

67936.

74.   The Laxey Wheel, named Isabella after Lady Isabella Hope, wife of Governor Hope, who opened it on 27 September 1854, is one of the great monuments of industrial archaeology in Britain. The wheel pumped water from the Laxey mines until 1920, was then purchased by the Manx government in 1965 and now, fully restored, provides an important tourist attraction. The wheel is 72 ft. 6ins. in diameter and was designed by the Manxman Robert Casement.

LAXEY GLEN GARDENS,

LAXEY, ISLE OF MAN.

This most Picturesque Glen is unsurpassed by any on the Island, and is Furnished complete with all the requisites of a Pleasure Ground.

AMERICAN BOWLING SALOON.

BILLIARDS !   BILLIARDS !!

**Bowling-Green Free !   Quoits Free !   Lawn Tennis Free !
Swings Free !   Croquet Free !   Hobby Horses Free !**

A GOOD BRASS and STRING BAND

In attendance Daily during the Season.

ALES, WINES & SPIRITS

Of the Finest Quality, at Reasonable Charges.

Visitors staying at the Hotel have free access to the Grounds.

HOTEL TARIFF.

Board, including Bedroom and use of Public Room
per day 7s 0d
Or, per week, £2 5s.
Children under 14 years, Half-price.

Dinners in Private Rooms, from 2s 6d
Visitors' Servants' Board, per day 4s 0d
Private Sitting Room, for week £1 10s
Bedrooms, per night   ...   . from 2s to 3s 0d
Bedroom Fires, per night 0s 6d
Attendance, per day 1s 0d
Arrangements made for Wedding Breakfasts.

M. & T. FORRESTER,
PROPRIETORS.

75. The Island's scenic glens, especially at Sulby and Laxey, have always provided important tourist attractions. This 1890 advertisement for Laxey shows how well Victorian visitors were catered for.

76.   Open air dancing at Laxey Glen Gardens in about 1914. Laxey, especially after the electric tram service reached it in 1899, became very popular and famous for the sylvan atmosphere of the glen and its many amenities.

Douglas

77. The early Royal Mail Packet steamer *Tynwald* leaving Douglas, *c*.1840. On the left is Douglas Head and beyond is the town and harbour with the old Red Pier lighthouse erected in 1832.

78. Douglas Harbour and Bay from Douglas Head. On the left is the Camera Obscura, opened in 1887.

79. Douglas Head lighthouse in about 1900. It was built in 1892, replacing the original light erected in 1832.

80. The impressive Marine Drive Gateway, Douglas Head. Dated 1891, it demonstrates the persistence of the castellated style throughout the 19th century in the Island.

81. The steamship *Mona* approaching Douglas Harbour in the early years of this century.

82. The age of sail slowly giving way to steam in Douglas Harbour about 1900.

136. Arrival of Steamers, Douglas. I. O. M

83.   During the boom years of the traditional holiday in the Isle of Man, Douglas Harbour and Pier were frequently the scene of frantic activity when thousands of visitors swarmed off the steamboats and invaded Douglas in search of accommodation.

84.   The once popular *Empress Queen* off Douglas in about 1913. She was the last paddle steamer used by the Isle of Man Steam Packet Company. She was launched in 1897 and later wrecked on the Isle of Wight during the 1914-18 War.

85.   Holiday crowds and steamers at Victoria Pier, Douglas, in about 1900. The pier was built on part of the Pollack Rocks in 1872 and allowed docking at all states of the tide. By 1874 six boats were operating to Douglas with fares of 6 shillings to 12 shillings. The pier was extended to its present length in 1888.

Victoria Pier, Douglas, I. O. M.

86. Sir William Hillary (1771-1847), a Yorkshireman and founder of the Royal National Lifeboat Institution in 1824. Hillary settled in Douglas in 1808 and lived at Fort Anne on Douglas Head, originally the home of Buck Whalley and then an hotel before its unfortunate demolition in 1972.

87. The famous Tower of Refuge, designed by John Welch, which marks the treacherous rocks in Douglas Bay. The Tower was erected in 1832 by Sir William Hillary who was much concerned by the loss of seamen in local wrecks.

88.   Manx lifeboats assembled in Douglas Bay on 10 May 1932 to mark the centenary of the R.N.L.I.

89. The ferry *Peveril* in Douglas Harbour. From 1962, the introduction of vehicle ferries did much to stimulate both holiday and commercial traffic to the Isle of Man. Car arrivals rose from 6,539 in 1962 to 23,600 thirteen years later.

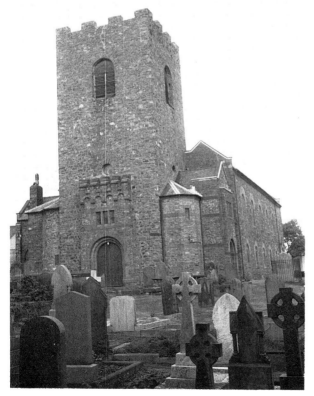

90. The rugged exterior of St George's, Douglas, conceals a galleried interior dating from about 1780 with Corinthian columns. The design is said to derive from the Georgian St James's, Whitehaven (1752), but restoration took place in 1910 when a chancel was added. The first chaplain of St George's was Charles Crebbin (1781-1817), and there is a memorial to the Manx marine biologist Edward Forbes in the church.

91. Old St Matthew's, built by Bishop Wilson in 1708, formerly stood by the Market (North Quay) and was part of a picturesque area of old Douglas. A new St Matthew's by J. L. Pearson opened in 1897 on a nearby site.

92. The *Castle Mona Hotel*, now surrounded by modern development, was erected in 1804 as the residence of the Governor, John Murray, later 4th Duke of Atholl. Both the architect, George Stewart, and the building materials employed were perhaps predictably imported from Scotland.

93. John Robinson's most distinguished contribution to Manx architecture is the Oddfellows Hall, Athol Street, erected in 1840-41. During the 1850s it served as a theatre, the Prince of Wales, and in 1860 was acquired by the Manx Government and became the Court House.

94. The Manx Government Office, Prospect Hill, was originally designed as the Bank of Mona in 1855 by John Robinson. The bank closed in 1880 and the building was then acquired by the Tynwald. It is a fine example of the late Regency style, with strong Italianate influence and handsome stucco detail.

95. Henry Brougham Loch (1827-1900) and his family. Loch served in the Crimean War and later became an enlightened and popular Governor of Man, 1863-82. Loch was created a peer in 1895 and his name is commemorated in the Loch Promenade, built in 1876-78.

96. The handsome stucco National Westminster Bank, Prospect Hill, Douglas. The building was formerly Dumbell's Bank whose failure on 3 February 1900 ('Black Saturday') proved to be one of the greatest disasters to hit the Isle of Man. George Dumbell was a Deemster for 18 years and a director of the Laxey mines. In 1887 he presented the Jubilee Clock (Victoria Street) to the people of Douglas.

97. The Renaissance style Town Hall, Ridgeway Street, Douglas, designed by Arthur Ardron in 1897. The building includes the Public Library and originally a fire station. The cost of construction was nearly £14,000.

98. The stylish Manx Museum building at Crellin's Hill was originally Noble's Hospital, erected in 1886 by Cubbon & Bleakley. P. M. C. Kermode was the first curator in 1922, followed by William Cubbon in 1932 who built up the valuable library and collections on Manx history.

99. The extension to the Manx Museum, Douglas, nearing completion in 1988. The building, designed by Ronnie Fell, is embellished by a course of sculptural designs in concrete by Daniel Gilbert of Ballaugh, representing aspects of Manx life of all periods mainly in a Celtic idiom. The new building will include a lecture theatre, art gallery and a special display video on Manx history.

100.   Holiday crowds on the Loch Promenade in about 1910. On the left is one of the Upper Douglas Tramway cars which operated a route via Victoria Street, Villa Marina and Broadway during the period 1896-1929, using Dick Kerr winding gear.

101.   The once prestigious *Villiers Hotel* is a key building on the Loch Promenade, and also in the identity of Douglas sea front. In 1988 the hotel, together with the buildings as far as Regent Street, are threatened with demolition.

102.   Late Victorian beach scene at Douglas Bay with a fine array of bathing machines. Note the undeveloped northern section of the seafront. In the centre is Castle Mona, and above, the *Falcon Cliff Hotel* with its large ballroom, since demolished.

103.   In calm weather Douglas Bay is idyllic but with an easterly, south-easterly or north-easterly gale the sea can become very rough and provide an exciting spectacle. Towards the centre can be seen the Methodist church, now rebuilt in modern style.

Douglas Head, I. O. M.

104. Typical pre-First World War crowds enjoying the view on Douglas Head.

EARLE HOUSE,

19, LOCH PROMENADE,

MRS. RILEY,

(OF RUNCORN),

PROPRIETRESS,

EARLE HOUSE

TERMS MODERATE,

On Application to

MISS RAYNER, Manageress.

105. Victorian boarding house advertisement for Earle House, Loch Promenade, Douglas. The *Villiers Hotel* is on the left.

106. Okell's Falcon Brewery, Falcon Street, Douglas, erected by William Okell in 1857. It is now the only surviving brewery on the Isle and a fine example of the local stucco style.

107. The first modern place of Roman Catholic worship on the Isle of Man was St Bridget's chapel, opened in 1814 near the Nunnery on land given by its owner, Major Taubman. By 1841 there were some 600 catholics in Man and in August 1859 the church of St Mary of the Isle was opened by the Bishop of Beverley, Dr. Briggs, on Prospect Hill.

108. These fine stucco villas along the east side of Finch Road form an outstanding architectural group. Originally part of the Finch Hill Estate, they were designed by John Robinson in about 1854. A distinctive feature is the treatment of the large gables as pediments with eave brackets.

109. An elegant doorway in Mount Pleasant with inset columns and fanlight, a tasteful ensemble amounting to a local style of which numerous examples still survive.

110. Attractive local vernacular style in 19th-century houses at the junction of Woodburn Square and Hawarden Avenue. Note the stucco hood moulds and highly decorative bargeboards. Stucco hood or drip moulds became a characteristic feature of Manx house design in the 19th century.

W. J. RENNISON,

Architect

AND

SURVEYOR,

4, 5 & 6 VILLIERS CHAMBERS,

DOUGLAS.

Plans, Specifications, Bills of Quantities and Measurements of Works executed on Reasonable Terms.

✦ARCHITECT FOR✦

The Falcon Cliff, Derby Castle, Grand Buildings, Athol and Regent Hotels, and most of the Principal Hotels and Boarding Houses in Douglas and other Towns of the Island.

111. Advertisement, *c.*1885, by W. J. Rennison, one of the main architects responsible for the development of Victorian Douglas. It lists some of the firm's achievements.

112. Demesne Road, Upper Douglas, an excellent example of late 19th-century boarding house development with attractive stucco decoration.

113. Rosemount or Trinity Methodist church, Bucks Road, was opened in June 1886 and designed by W. Waddington of Burnley. The spire, added in 1911, is a distinctive landmark. To the right is the *Rosemount Hotel*, part of a John Robinson terrace, with later embellishments to the original design.

114.   Destruction of the fine late Regency style terrace on Mount Havelock in August 1988. The terrace formed an integral part of the Mona Terrace and Finch Road area.

115.   Outstanding among Manx entertainment buildings is the Gaiety Theatre which possesses a superb interior designed by the great Frank Matcham. The theatre was converted from the Marina Pavilion (1893), opened with *The Telephone Girl*, and later often produced dramatised versions of Hall Caine's novels.

Programme.

Grand Opening Monday, July 16, 1900.

FOR SIX NIGHTS ONLY

MISS ADA BLANCHE,

FROM DRURY LANE THEATRE,

Supported by her Own Company of London Artistes.

Chorus of Telephone Girls and Special Dancers.

Special Production of the Successful Musical Comedy—

The Telephone Girl!

Libretto by Sir Augustus Harris, F. C. Burnand and A. Sturgess.
Music by Gaston Serpette and James M. Glover.

Dick Wimple ... (Clerk in Banking House of Hobbs)...Mr W. R. SHIRLEY
Sylvester Bartrum (General Inspector of Telegraphs)...Mr J. A. THOMSON
Bartholomew Pilchard...(Farmer from Cornwall, formerly in Militia under
          Gen. Sir George Jellaby) ...   . Mr C. WHITE
Murray Anne   ...   . (his Wife)... Miss LIZZIE CLAREMONT
Dolly Dobbs (their Niece, known in London as " Belle Bell," the
          Unrivalled Variety Sparkler) ...   Miss JENNIE ARMSTRONG
Prince Imatoff ...   ... (a Russian Nobleman)...Mr L. CORY-THOMAS
James ... (Footman in Service of Belle Bell) ... Mr ROLANDO MARTIN
Miss Berry McNabb (Superintendent of Telephone Department)...
                                        Miss BELLE LYTHAM
Nellie ...   .(Lottie's Friend)...   ...Miss MURIEL VOX
Lottie ...   ... **(The Telephone Girl)** ...   **Miss ADA BLANCHE**

Pollie...	...	...		... ... Miss ALICE JAMES
Maudie	...	...		... ... Miss BELLA LEWIS
Edie ...	...	...		... Miss LILLIAN LILFORD
Ella ...	...	...		... Miss MAY BROOKE
Katie...	...	...		... ... Miss LOUIE LILLIAN
Lizzie...	...	...		... ... Miss HARRIET TIDD
Minnie	...	...	Telephone	... ... Miss MARY GOODE
Fanny	...	...	Girls.	Miss BEATRICE LLEWELLYN
Janie...	...	...		...Miss CONSTANCE LILFORD
Gertie	...	...		... Miss FANNIE RUSSELL
Susie...	...	...		... ... Miss DORA WEBER
Nora...	...	...		... Miss ETHEL THORNE
Florrie	...	...		... ... Miss NITA RAYE
Lucy ...	...	...		... ... Miss MILLIE ROSS

ACT I. ... ... THE TELEPHONE OFFICE
NOTE.—This Scene is an Exact Representation of the Telephone Exchange, London.
PAS DE DEUX by Misses DORA WEBER and ETHEL THORNE.

ACT II. ...   . DRAWING ROOM AT BELLE BELL'S
DANCERS by the Misses FANNIE RUSSELL, DORA WEBER,
          and ETHEL THORNE.
SONG—"The Rare Fair Maid," written and composed by Clifton Bingham, sung by
          kind permission of Messrs Francis, Day and Hunter.

Proprietors -   -   -   - The Palace and Derby Castle, Limited.
Manager and Secretary—Mr. CHAS FOX, Junr. | Acting Manager—HAROLD GOLDING.

116. Programme for the Grand Opening of the Gaiety Theatre, Douglas, on 16 July 1900.

117.   One of the plaster figures forming part of the attractive Baroque interior of Frank Matcham's Gaiety Theatre. The theatre was taken over by the Manx government in 1976, and carefully restored to its former glory in consultation with Victor Glasstone.

118. The former entrance to the Palace entertainment centre, Queen's Promenade, Douglas. This attractive and typical seaside building was demolished to make way for the concrete Casino.

119. Interior of the Palace Ballroom, Douglas, in about 1910. 'Monster' ballrooms became a feature of entertainment in the late 19th century, often as part of pleasure grounds. The Palace was the last – built in 1889 and restored after a fire in 1921, it has space for 6,000 dancers.

THE PALACE

AND

NEW OPERA HOUSE.

ACKNOWLEDGED by one and all to be the Largest, Brightest, and Most Popular Amusement Resort in Douglas.

GRAND
VOCAL & INSTRUMENTAL CONCERTS

Every Afternoon from 3 to 5, by the Most Talented Artists of the Day.

High-Class
VARIETY ENTERTAINMENTS

Every Evening, in the

NEW OPERA HOUSE.

The Cream of Variety Talent from the Leading London and Provincial Halls.

DANCING

Every Evening, from 7-30 to 11 p.m., in the

GRAND PAVILION.

The Largest in the World—with the Finest Floor, 18,000 feet of Polished Oak.

SACRED CONCERT

EVERY SUNDAY EVENING.

SUPERB ORCHESTRA.—32 PERFORMERS.

Magnificent Gardens and Woodland Slopes.

ADMISSION—Up to 6 p.m., 6d, After—1s.

120. Advertisement for the 'Palace and New Opera House', Douglas, published in 1892. The Palace was opened as 'the largest ballroom in Europe' in 1889.

121. The Palace Lido, formerly the Palace, opened as the Colosseum in July 1913, costing £11,000. The Edwardian Baroque design was by George Kaye.

122. Derby Castle, a fine marine villa in the romantic castellated style, was built in 1836 and belonged at one time to the Pollock family. In 1877 it opened as an entertainment centre with a theatre and large ballroom and became a popular rendezvous. In 1971 the Castle was demolished and replaced by the concrete Summerland complex and Aquadrome.

VILLA MARINA,
DOUGLAS. I.O.M.

123.   The Villa Marina, a major seaside development costing £16,000 and designed by Robinson & Jones (Leeds), opened in July 1913. During 1929-31 a related Marina Colonnade was added by B. Prentice Morgan. A £3.5 million refurbishment for the Marina has recently been announced.

124.   The narrow tiled facade of the former Strand Cinema with flanking turrets and leaded coloured glass windows. It remains an important survival of cinema design, opened on 2 August 1913, and later reconstructed in 1930, possibly by Harry Lomas.

125. Strand (originally Sand) Street is the most popular shopping thoroughfare in Douglas. This view shows two former cinemas, the Tudor style Picture House and, beyond, the turreted Strand. Both are now closed.

126. The Royalty Cinema, Walpole Avenue, with its moulded white ceramic tiles, was designed by Harry Lomas on the site of the old timber Pier Pavilion in 1927. On the right is the Douglas Sea Terminal, designed by Davidson Marsh & Co. and T. H. Kennaught, and opened by Princess Margaret on 6 July 1965.

ROYALTY CINEMA

WALPOLE AVENUE
(Close to Horse and Bus Terminus).

****

Even if you are not a Picture "Fan" you must
not fail to see

The LAST WORD in Picture Houses

THE ROYALTY

Accommodates in perfect comfort nearly 1,200 patrons.
Artistic decorations in modern style; scientific ven-
tilating and heating installations; luxuriously up-
holstered seating; costly electric lighting and perfect
projection of Pictures by the most up-to-date machines
and plant. There is no better or more comfortable
Picture House anywhere.

THE

Big Super-Talkies are Here !

Continuous Programme from 6-30. (Sundays, 8-15.)

On Wet Days — Mornings, 10-30; Afternoons, 2-30.

Popular Prices—6d., 1/-, 1/6, and 1/9.

Our Motto: "If it's good, it's here; if it's here, it's
good."

127. Advertisement for the Royalty Cinema, Walpole Avenue, in about 1932.

128.   In 1929-30 a major new cinema, the Crescent, was built on the seafront. It was designed by Harry Lomas using the characteristic Art Deco white tiling for the facade and a less common pierced balustrade around the top. The now much altered building functions as a 'Family Leisure Centre'.

129.   Joseph Cunningham (1853-1924) from Liverpool founded his famous holiday camp in the Isle of Man, first at Laxey in 1892, moving to the Howstrake Estate (Groudle Glen) in 1903, and finally to Little Switzerland in 1904. The camp was a great innovative success and in the mid-1930s averaged over 60,000 men per season and made an annual profit of around £37,000.

130. Humorous publicity postcard issued by Cunningham's Camp in about 1900. In 1914 the camp was used for internees, and during the 1939-45 War it became H.M.S. *St George* for naval training. In 1945 it was sold and continued to be used for holidays until later building development occupied the site.

131. A meeting in progress at the former racecourse at Belle Vue. This once popular place of amusement closed down in 1929.

132. An historic photograph of the opening by the Duke of Sutherland of the Isle of Man Railway at Douglas on 1 July 1873. The Peel line began in 1873, followed by Port Erin in 1874. A separate Northern Railway Company opened a Peel-Ramsey section in 1879.

Manx Railways, I·o·M

11390

133. A steam train about to leave Douglas station in about 1920. The photograph shows the 1887 station buildings and the former platform canopy. Since the war, the station area has been curtailed on the south side.

134. The electric tram terminus near Derby Castle (now Summerland) in about 1910, showing the original iron canopy over the station.

135.   Much the same view of the Electric Railway terminus in 1988. The iron canopies have gone, and the attractive Derby Castle has given way to the concrete mass of Summerland.

136.   In 1960 two ex-County Donegal diesel railcars were purchased to run winter services on the Manx steam railway. The cars are seen here at Douglas station where they are now used for shunting.

137. The horse tram depot at Summerland at the northern end of Douglas Bay. In 1988 some 80 horses were owned by the tramway, and each animal is given careful training before going into service.

138. The famous and ever popular horse trams provide a pleasant and sedate means of transport along Douglas promenade during the summer. The service was begun by Thomas Lightfoot (from Sheffield) in 1876 and later acquired by Douglas Corporation in 1900. Some 80 horses are used, and retired animals are cared for at Bulrhenny, Richmond Hill, Douglas.

139. Changing ends at Victoria Street. A pleasant feature of the horse trams is that the horses seem to be as keen to pull the trams as the visitors are to ride in them!

140. Electric Railway car no. 2, with trailer, approaching the Summerland terminus. The 3ft.-gauge line opened in 1893, linking Douglas and Laxey and the original trams are still in use, making it of great interest to transport enthusiasts. The line was extended to Ramsey in 1899.

141. The new Tourist Trophy Grandstand in Glencrutchery Road, Douglas, was opened by the Duke of Kent on 6 June 1986, at a cost of £480,000. The first races were held on 28 May 1907 and since then have given the Isle of Man world prominence in motor-cycle racing and important financial benefit.

142.   Spectators and riders at an evening practice at the Grandstand, Glencrutchery Road, prior to the 1988 TT Races.

143.   Rally motor-cyclists enjoying a somewhat hectic race circuit arranged on the sands at Douglas Bay in September 1988. This new attraction draws large crowds and began in the mid-1980s.

Braddan

144. Old Kirk Braddan, mother church of Douglas, remains an almost unaltered example of a Georgian auditory church with box pews, three-decker pulpit, gallery and Decalogue. A collection of Norse and Celtic crosses is preserved in the church. The photograph shows the tower added in 1773, and George Stewart's striking obelisk to Lord Henry Murray, son of the Duke of Atholl (d.1805).

145.   A well attended open air service at new Braddan church, *c.*1920. This tradition has persisted for many years with congregations sometimes numbering over one thousand, especially between the Wars, when many were holidaymakers.

146.   In March 1869 it was decided to build a new church at Kirk Braddan from designs by John Loughborough Pearson, using local stone. The builders were Wall & Hook (of Brinscombe, Somerset) and the cost was £4,300. The tower (1883-6) originally had a spire but this has gone, having been twice destroyed by storms.

The Nunnery

147. Romney's portrait of Captain John Taubman
(1746-1822) in 1788. He was a son of 'the great
Taubman' of the Nunnery, and later became a Major in
the Manx Defensibles and Speaker of the House of Keys.

148. The Nunnery, named from a fragment of
St Bridget's Nunnery suriviving nearby, was designed
for the Goldie-Taubman family by John Pinch of Bath
in 1823. The Inkerman Obelisk has been modified
after storm damage a few years ago.

Onchan

ONCHAN VILLAGE, I.O.M.

149.   Late 19th-century view of Onchan showing St Peter's church where Captain Bligh was married in 1781. On the left is Molly Carrooin's Cottage, a traditional Manx cottage, now preserved as a folk museum.

150. William Bligh, notorious as the harsh captain of the *Bounty*. In 1781 Bligh married, at Kirk Onchan, Elizabeth Betham, daughter of the first Customs Officer appointed by the British Excise in Man. Several Manxmen, including Fletcher Christian and Peter Heyward, were on the *Bounty* in 1789.

151. Government House (near Governors Bridge), originally Bemahague, was first rented (1863-82) by Governor Loch, and later purchased as an official residence in 1903. The west end was remodelled during 1903-1906.

Baillie Scott

152. The distinguished architect Mackay Hugh Baillie Scott (1865-1945) was born near
Ramsgate, educated at Worthing and articled to C. E. Davis (city architect of Bath) 1886-9.
He settled in Douglas in 1889, working for a local surveyor Fred Saunderson at no. 7, Athol
Street. In 1893 Scott set up his own practice and occupied the Red House in Victoria Road,
Douglas, which he had designed in 1892.

Within the drawing:

·Ground Plan·

·HOUSE·
NOW·IN·COURSE·OF·ERECTION·
GLENCRUTCHERY·DOUGLAS·
ISLE·OF·MAN·

M·H·B·Scott·
Architect

153.   Baillie Scott's drawing of the Red House, Victoria Road (*Building News*, April 1893). The foundation stone (left of the main door) bears the date 20 October 1892, and the site was purchased from Deemster Thomas Kneen, a close and influential friend of the architect.

154. Baillie Scott's Red House in 1987 – now perhaps the best preserved of all his buildings and carefully maintained by its present owners.

155. The roughcast Arts and Crafts style Village Hall at Onchan is an important early work (1897-8) by Baillie Scott, showing Charles Voysey's influence. Later it influenced buildings on the continent and was praised by Muthesius and others.

156. Ivydene in Little Switzerland is one of Baillie Scott's best houses in the Isle of Man but it is now much altered. Commanding a cliff-edge view over Douglas Bay, the house was built in 1893-4 for Richard M. Kerruish.

157. The handsome stucco villa 'Ashfield' in Glencrutchery Road dates from about 1850 and was at one time occupied by the Gelling family. The photograph shows the west side with the sympathetically enlarged porch designed by Baillie Scott in the mid-1890s.

158.   Members of the Gelling family enjoying afternoon tea in the garden of Ashfield House in the 1890s.

159.   Around 1905 Captain William J. Crebbin left Douglas and moved to West Sussex where he built the second Ashfield (*above*) at East Preston. He lived here until 1933 with his wife Clara, daughter of Edward Gelling (d.1913) of Ashfield, Glencrutchery Road, Onchan. Captain Anthony Crebbin (grandson) now lives at Ashfield, Salamander Bay, New South Wales.

Manx Miscellany

160. Cooil Methodist chapel, built in 1870 by the Gelling family, replaced the building on the other side of the road, said to be the oldest Methodist chapel on the Island. The original chapel was constructed in 1796 and rebuilt in 1834.

161. The now disused Dalrymple Memorial chapel at Union Mills. Designed by John Robinson in 1862, it commemorated the Congregationalist James Dalrymple, a deacon at the Finch Hill chapel.

162. Crosby Methodist chapel, a delightful essay in turreted gothic of about 1840, with a later porch.

LORD of the Isle that breeds the tailless cats,
Tis his to teach—and ours to learn who can—
"The proper study of mankind," and that's
The Masterpiece of Man.

163. Sir Thomas Hall Caine (1853-1931), author of several popular novels set in the Isle of Man, including *The Deemster* (1887) and *The Eternal City* (1901). He was of Manx and Cumberland parentage and belonged to a circle that included D.G. Rossetti, Baillie Scott, John Ruskin and others.

GREEBA CASTLE, SIR AND LADY HALL CAINE ON STEPS.

164. Greeba Castle near Crosby was designed in 1849 by John Robinson for William Nowell and was originally called Ashburn. In 1895 the writer Hall Caine rented the property and purchased it the following year. Several notable people stayed at the Castle as his guests including Ruskin, Rossetti, Archibald Knox and Baillie Scott.

165. Proud owner of Greeba Castle, Mr. Hall Caine, author, man of letters and Manx patriot, here looking very much the part!

166. The new *Summit Hotel*, Snaefell, which opened in August 1906 in response to the increasing success of the Mountain Railway. The hotel was badly damaged by fire in 1982, and restored in a plainer style. At first (1893) it cost 2s. return from Laxey to enjoy the wonderful mountain view, compared with £3.50 in 1988.

167. The picturesque Groudle Glen Railway (2 ft. gauge) opened in 1896, running down the Glen to a sea lion and polar bear enclosure. The line closed in 1962 but owing to determined efforts by volunteers, re-opened in 1985. Of the two locomotives, the original *Sea Lion* is now fully restored (by British Nuclear Fuels, Sellafield), and *Polar Bear* is at Amberley Chalk Pits Museum, Sussex.

168. Ballasalla in about 1910. Since the 12th century, the village has been associated with the nearby Rushen Abbey and stands at the entrance of the Silverdale Glen. The industrial expansion at Ronaldsway may well affect Ballasalla's seclusion in the future.

169. Ronaldsway airport in 1988. Regular air services began in the early 1930s, and during the 1939-45 War the site became a gunnery school and Royal Naval Air Station (H.M.S. Urley). New terminal buildings by T. H. Kennaugh were opened in June 1953.

Select Bibliography

Birch, Jack W., *The Isle of Man: a study in economic geography*, C.U.P., 1964.

Boyd, J.I.C., *The Isle of Man Railway*, 2nd ed., 1968.

Chappell, Connery, *The Dumbell Affair*, Merseyside, T. Stephenson, Prescott, 1981.

Chappell, Connery, *Island Lifeline*, Mersyside, T. Stephenson, Prescott, 1980. Marking the 150th anniversary of the Isle of Man Steam Packet Co. Ltd.

Chappell, Connery, *Island of barbed wire: Internment on the Isle of Man in World War Two*, Corgi Books, 1984. First ed. Robert Hale, 1984.

Corran, H.S., *The Isle of Man*, David & Charles, 1977.

Cregeen, Archibald, *A Dictionary of the Manks Language*, Douglas, 1835. Reprinted in 1969.

Cubbon, William, *Bibliography of the Literature of the Isle of Man*, 2 vols., 1933-39.

Cumming, J.G., *The Great Stanley; or James, seventh Earl of Derby*, 1867.

Fell, Christine, *et al.* (ed.), *The Viking Age in the Isle of Man*, Select Papers 9th Viking Conference ... Isle of Man, 1981. Viking Soc. for Northern Research & University College, London, 1983.

Garrad, L.S., *et al.*, *The Industrial Archaeology of the Isle of Man*, David & Charles, 1972.

Haining, Samuel, *A Historical Sketch and Descriptive view of the Isle of Man*, Douglas, 1822.

Harrison, S., *100 Years of Heritage: the work of the Manx Museum and National Trust*, Manx Museum, 1986.

Henry, F., *Ships of the Isle of Man Steam Packet Co.*, Glasgow, 1962.

Holliday, Bob, *Racing round the Island: a Manx Tale of Speed on Wheels*, David & Charles, 1976.

Jespersen, A., *The Lady Isabella Waterwheel of the Great Laxey Mining Co., Isle of Man, 1854-1954*, Copenhagen, 1954.

Keble, Rev. John, *Life of Thomas Wilson, D.D., Lord Bishop of Sodor and Man*, 2 vols., Oxford, J.H. Parker, 1863.

Kermode, P.M.C., *Manx Crosses or the inscribed & sculptured monuments of the Isle of Man*, Bemrose, 1907.

Kermode, P.M.C., 'Ship-burial in the Isle of Man (at Knoc-y-Doonee)', in *Antiquaries Journal*, vol. x, 1930.

Kerrvish, D.W., *The Manx Cat*, 3rd ed., 1964.

Kinvig, R.H., *The Isle of Man: a Social, Cultural and Political History*, Liverpool University Press, 1975. First ed. 1944.

Kneen, John J., *Place names of the Isle of Man*, 6 vols., Douglas, 1925-29.

Kneen, John J., *The Personal names of the Isle of Man*, O.U.P., 1937.

Manx Museum and National Trust, *The Ancient and Historic Monuments of the Isle of Man: a general guide*, 5th ed., Douglas, 1981.

Moore, T.M., 'Architectural and Social aspects of Douglas 1595-1900', in *Isle of Man Natural History and Antiquarian Soc.*, vol. viii (New Series) No. 2, 1979.

Munich, P.A. (ed.), *Chronica Regnum Manniae et Insularum*, Manx Soc. vols. 22 and 23, 1874. With English translation. Main source of early history of the Isle of Man.

Pearson, F.K., *Isle of Man Tramways*, David & Charles, 1970.

Radcliffe, Constance, *Ramsey 1600-1800*, Douglas, 1986.

Stenning, Ernest H., *Portrait of the Isle of Man*, 4th ed., Hale, 1978.

Train, Joseph, *An historical and statistical account of the Isle of Man from the earliest times*, 2 vols., Douglas, 1845.

The original appearance of King William's College (Hansom and Welch, 1830) before the fire of 1844. The college was built on the Hangohill estate with money from the Bishop Barrow fund. The college was built from Castletown limestone from the Scarlett quarry.